T0129991

HOW MANY
Summers?

A Look at Life through Ordinary Eyes

WADE MCGAULEY

BALBOA.
PRESS

A DIVISION OF HAY HOUSE

Balboa Press books may be ordered through
booksellers or by contacting:

Balboa Press
A Division of Hay House
1663 Liberty Drive
Bloomington, IN 47403
www.balboapress.com.au
1 (877) 407-4847

Print information available on the last page.

ISBN: 978-1-5043-0231-9 (sc)
ISBN: 978-1-5043-0232-6 (e)

Balboa Press rev. date: 05/12/2016

To Mum and Dad

And to a few special people:
J ... T ... K ... N ... E ... S ... R ... L
You know who you are.

Thank you for your guidance, support, and love.

You may say I'm a dreamer, but I'm not the only one.

—*John Lennon*

CONTENTS

ACKNOWLEDGMENTS

I would first like to say that my opinions in this book are just that—my opinions. Discussion about these life issues is welcome, and I would love to hear your thoughts.

I am just an ordinary guy, finding my way through life like everybody else. I do not have any formal training in human behaviour or psychology. I've just gained a bit of wisdom from observing people, witnessing events, and realizing we all have many of the same problems. I guess it's just a matter of how we deal with them and how we perceive the world.

I would like to thank everyone who encouraged me to put pen to paper—everyone who has crossed my path on this journey and the many more to come.

To all the people I have shared my emotions with and the special ones I have given my heart and love too ... you know who you are. For all the conversations about the mysteries of life that I have been fascinated about, thanks for listening. We do have a precious life.

To two people I admire from their teachings and talks, Dr. Wayne Dyer and Lama Marut—thank you for showing me that happiness can be achieved, that love can be wonderful, and that compassion and kindness exist.

To everybody who helped put this book together, I can't thank you enough. The guidance and encouragement I have been given to get me through this process is overwhelming.

To all the great musicians I have listened to, thank you for your creativity, your words, and your talent, and for inspiring joy and emotions through song.

The world really is a beautiful place. We all have to play our part with peace, love, and happiness.

How Many Summers?

Summer breeze, makes me feel fine,
Blowing through the jasmine in my mind.

—*Seals and Crofts*

M ost of us at some point in our lives have felt like the little mouse running around and around on that wheel, getting nowhere. We just want to hop off and reassess our lives. We may ask ourselves the famous questions: What is life? Why am I here? Is this all there is? We may feel consumed by work, money, and relationships, often getting what we don't want and not getting what we do.

I was inspired to write this book after many years of working in the hospitality and service industry. I spoke to many people over this time, including family, friends, and strangers. I learned a lot about human behaviour, and I guess I gained a little wisdom along the way. Through it all, I came to realise one thing: each of us has a precious human life.

I once read that in the Western world, the average lifespan is about seventy-five years. But in reality, our departure from this earth can come at any time. We really don't think of it much, or we believe it always happens to somebody else. We are in denial.

When I was a child, I used to love summer. It was a holiday, so the beach and fun took up most of my time. One day would drift into another, and soon it would be back to school all over again. Each year passed very quickly.

If we really think about it, we see that we cannot predict how many summers we may have left. Maybe we should try to embrace every day, face our fears, and show some kindness and a bit more love. Let's enjoy the journey and ask ourselves, "How many summers do I have?"

There is no time to waste. Let go and enjoy. The past is gone, and the future is not here yet. All we have is the now.

Birth

When a child is born into this world,
it has no concept of the tone the skin it's living in.

—*Nenah Cherry*

The miracle of birth. We have all experienced it. Yes, even you. You arrived …

After the first breath, the journey begins. Once you were not here; now you are. Take a few moments to think about that. Birth is truly amazing.

Of course, we all know we are born after our mother and father engage in intercourse and form a union. Pregnancy takes place, but the beginning of a new life cannot really be explained. It's still a mystery.

New babies need everything done for them. They must be fed, sheltered, bathed, and most of all, loved and protected. I guess after being looked after for so long and having everything done for them, as soon as they develop, they try to be older and to show adults they can do things for themselves. You will understand what I mean if you ask a five-year-old child, "How old are you?" On most occasions, the answer will be "I am five, but I am nearly six." Try it.

It's kind of funny that from an early age, we want to project ourselves into the future and to be older. This goes on into our teen years. Kids will always say, "I wish I were a teenager. Then I'd get to do stuff—cool stuff like an adult." A twelve-year-old can't wait to be thirteen, and the thirteen can't wait to be sixteen. Then the eighteen-year-old of course wants to be twenty-one. Can you see where I am heading here?

At some point, a shift in thought occurs, and age gets looked at and talked about differently. When we get older, we often start saying things like, "Where have all the years gone?" or "Everything has gone so fast."

When we are young, we wish to be older, but most adults when ageing may wish to be more youthful. Time moves very quickly. It really is a short life, as people say. The only way to look at it both ways—either young or old—is to try to accept where you are in that moment. After all, we cannot stop time.

Ageing happens to all of us. Encourage young people to enjoy the age they are—to be children while they can—because adulthood will soon approach. As for us adults, we can resolve to treat each day as if it were our last, because I've got news for all of us: one day it will be.

Reassessing what is important in your life may help you stop putting off things you wish to do. Maybe you will face some of your fears or take some risks, or find your purpose or things you enjoy. Don't be so hard on yourself. Try helping others, and be kind. Showing a bit more compassion and love can work wonders, not just for everyone else but also for you.

Embrace this special event called birth. Be grateful you are having a human experience or a spiritual one. However you are looking at it, give it all you've got.

Ageing

I taught myself how to grow
Now I'm crooked on the outside,
And the inside's broke.

—Ryan Adams

Wade McGauley

I was once sitting in a café in Hawaii. As I sat there drinking my green tea, a tour bus pulled up to the curb. Out jumped about ten boys and girls in their early twenties. All of them were fit and healthy, their bodies in prime condition. A moment later, another bus arrived, and getting out of it were much older citizens, the years showing in their faces and bodies.

As I watched the activities of these two groups, I went into deep thought. Those older folks were once like the young group, and the young will be like the old. It struck me that this is the cycle of life. But we never contemplate this in our youth.

A wise person once said, "We are born. We age. We get sick. And we die." Hard-hitting stuff, I know. But hey, it sounds like the truth to me. Ageing comes to us all. Each day we are changing. We try to prolong our lives, but there is no magic potion to stop death. We may be able to slow it down a fraction by looking after ourselves—eating right, exercising, de-stressing, or even Botox-ing—but it will get us all in the end.

So the only thing I've got to say is, "Don't fight it. Embrace it." It's all part of the process of life. Use the little wisdom you gain along the way. There is nothing else to do, and no need to worry.

Health and Fitness

I feel good.
I knew that I would.
I feel good. I knew that I would now.
So good, so good.

—James Brown

If we are going to enjoy our time on this planet, my friends, maybe we should feel good about it and about ourselves. If you were given a fully functional body, you should be able move around in a free and natural way. I like to think of our cars in this case to give an example of what I am trying to get at here. Our cars get us from A to B, which is similar to what our bodies do in our day-to-day activities.

Sometimes we look after our cars with more care than we do our bodies. We get our cars serviced to keep them running smoothly. We change the oil. We fill them with fuel and wash them. (Well, not all of us wash them …) Meanwhile, most of us neglect our bodies. We don't refuel them with the right food and liquid. We let them get run down and sick.

Unfortunately, unlike our cars, we cannot trade our bodies in. However, if we are mindful and make a few adjustments, we can feel more vibrant and energetic. Change of lifestyle can only come from our inner thoughts and discipline. Small steps and changing habits bring big results. It's best to check with a doctor, nutritionist, or fitness expert to get started or educated.

In the Western world, most of us have access to fresh food and water. Sometimes we become lazy and take the easy options, like fast fatty foods, too much sugar, and little or no exercise. Think before you refuel your body. Most eating and drinking patterns are habits, and of course, habits can be broken.

It takes a combination of things for this to happen: willpower, getting help from the right sources, wanting to change, encouragement, and your own thought process. Lack of motivation, laziness, lifestyle choices, and many other excuses can arise. It's up to you in the end to make the change required. Take responsibility for your own actions and health. Don't blame others, and take healthy steps if this is the direction in which you wish to go.

If you would like to feel and even look better, keep your body moving with some form of exercise. Find something you like doing, such as swimming, jogging, going to the gym, and walking. No excuses. You can find something. Just do it. Your body and mind will appreciate it.

Small adjustments to diet and exercise can bring great results. Mobility improves, a feeling of wellness develops, and a sense of happiness arises. Yes, you have a choice, just like you do with your car. You can look after it or wait until it falls apart.

Be good to yourself. Diets and fads come and go. Come on, we have seen them all. I think it really comes down to common sense about food and drink, don't you think? Consult an expert if you are not sure or need help. Simple things like lean meats, fish, plenty of vegetables, fruit, nuts, seeds, and smaller portions might be a good start. Plenty of water and of course chocolate, plenty of chocolate … sorry, I got bit carried away there.

Really, it just comes down to common sense about lifestyle and diets. Everything in moderation, and enjoy it. Break out the treats and your favourite foods every now and then. Enjoy a few drinks with good company and laugh a lot. That's about it.

Breath

Sometimes, all I need is the air that I breathe and to love you.—The Hollies

D o we ever really think about our breathing on a daily basis? We need breath for survival; oxygen supplies the body with its most vital nutrient. Yet because breathing occurs automatically, we are not very conscious of it.

We'll do an activity like running and say, "I am out of breath," or do an activity like swimming and hold our breath underwater, but on most occasions, we never think about our breath. It just happens, in and out, in and out. On most occasions, our breaths are very shallow and fast. This is due mainly to our lifestyles. We hurry a lot, stress too much, and have anxiety and problems to deal with.

Modern technology also plays a big part. We tend to spend more time inside on our devices, and this stops us from exercising and getting fresh air, breathing deeply, and clearing our lungs. Deep breathing nourishes our bodies, giving us more energy and vitality. Shallow breathing, on the other hand, can lead to health issues and lack of energy.

Try deep breathing every now and then; it will relax you. When you're overthinking or feeling overwhelmed, tense, and uneasy, turn to deep breathing. It's a simple but effective tool we can all call upon. It can be done anywhere.

Next time you're angry or tense, consider how you are breathing. Maybe slow it down a little, using conscious deep breathing, and bring yourself back to calmness. Even in the car stopped at traffic lights, breathe in a few times and release tension from your body. Just make sure you move when the light turns green.

Be aware of your breathing at different times of the day. Check your emotions and feelings at the same time. A few deep breaths may be all you need.

6

Death

> *Everybody wants to get to heaven,*
> *Everybody wants to get to heaven*
> *but nobody wants to die.*
>
> *—Stephen Cummings*

Okay, so nobody wants to read or hear about death, right? If you've gotten this far in my book, could you please read on? We really must be more open to the discussions about the end of our lives.

When I was young and my grandparents passed on, my parents never discussed it with me. It was hushed up and kept very secret. I went to the funeral, and it was quite confusing because all these people were there, some crying, all of them looking sad, and most of them whispering. I guess my parents were just trying to protect us kids and thinking we didn't need to understand this death stuff because it might affect the way we look at life.

Even back then, when I went to funerals and watched the coffin lowered into the ground, I wondered what happened to that person and where are he or she was going now. It was never discussed after the funerals, and our lives just went on. I look back now and wish we all had been a bit more open about it, reflected on it, and tried and understand the cycle of life and death.

If we look at the daily news, death is everywhere. When it's someone we don't know who passes, we disregard it very quickly. We may pause and reflect on it for a moment, but soon we get back to whatever we were doing. It takes the death of a family member, a friend, or a loved one to shake us to the core, and that's when reality hits.

When we do attend a funeral, it's about the only time we think of our mortality. It's not morbid to think of your own death every now and then. In fact, it can actually wake you up a bit, and you may realize you want to enjoy every moment you have.

Tomorrow could be your last day. So come on, my friends, embrace each day as it comes, no matter what it throws at you. Each moment you experience will come and go.

Of course, when you do experience a death of someone close to you, your heart breaks. Your emotions are clouded, and your life changes in seconds. You may become confused, upset, and even angry. The hurt can be unbearable. Losing someone we love brings pain and mental anguish.

Mourn the best way you know. Use your faith or spiritual beliefs, or obtain comfort from family and friends. Maybe think about what comes next for the departed. A better place maybe, peace, freedom ... whatever your thoughts are, wish them well. This may bring some comfort to you.

After the mourning process, however long it takes, reflect on that person's life and how you were part of it. A passing of this kind can bring you back to reality and truth. It can change your way of thinking, and you may well want to live life to the fullest and each day as your last, because one day it will be.

If you are born, you will die. That's a fact.

Look, I know this is not a great topic to think about, but we have to put it out there. Try not to worry too much about your day-to-day problems. Love your family, friends, and life in general. Everything goes in time; you only have now.

I keep saying it, but be content, show some loving kindness, laugh more, and seek happiness. This is a precious life we have; we may as well enjoy it, Who knows how much time we have left? We always think we have more time, but we don't.

Appreciate how brief life is. This can bring freedom. It can help you focus on being happy and present. Tomorrow is never promised. Give it your best shot.

A Personal Moment

Now there's a way and I know that I have to go away,
I know I have to go away.—Cat Stevens

On a wet Wednesday afternoon as I was driving home from work, an unusual feeling came over me. Two voices were fighting in my mind. One was telling me to go to the gym and get some exercise, and the other was saying to go home and get some rest.

I was feeling somewhat drained and tired. Just a few weeks before, my father had passed away, and the grieving process and my emotions about the whole thing were still with me. I decided at this time it was best for me to go home, rest, and reflect. As I lay on my bed reading, I could hear the thunder and rain. Before long, I was sound asleep.

A few hours passed, and I was awakened by a loud scratching sound that was coming from a screen attached to a balcony door in the next room. I lay there listening and decided I'd better investigate what this sound was. As I approached the door, a bird was trying to get in, with its claws attached to the screen door.

It was very dark outside because of the storm, and as I looked closely, this bird was quite distinct to me. Its colours and markings brought back some memories. The bird I was looking at was a cockatiel—a small breed of parrot. As I clicked the door open, the bird hopped onto the floor.

This was interesting. I thought, What do I do now? Do I push it away or try to bring it inside? The bird and I stared at each other for a few seconds. Instinct made me whistle at it. The bird chirped back. I repeated the whistle again. The bird chirped back again.

We stared at each other, and after a few moments, the bird took flight. I closed the door, went back inside my apartment, and sat on the couch. My heart was beating fast as I looked at a picture of my dad near my TV.

When my parents were alive, they lived out of the city, about a two-hour drive away. Mum had passed a few years earlier, and Dad lived alone in the house until he died. I sat there thinking about both of them and about this strange visit from my little bird friend.

After Mum passed, Dad's main companion was a bird. Yes, that's right—a cockatiel bird. Just to make things clear and a bit freakier, this type of bird does not just fly around the suburbs. Nobody I have asked has ever seen one do so.

Thoughts and emotions ran wild through my mind. Was this a message from Dad? A message from God? A higher force, maybe? Or was it just a coincidence? Who knows. I still don't know. The world we live in holds many mysteries.

I still think about that bird to this day. I laugh silently to myself sometimes, wondering if this was maybe a sign from Dad saying, "Hey, son, everything is okay, enjoy your life. Just letting you know all is good."

People have many different views about whether there is an afterlife. Do we go to heaven? Are we reborn? Do we just turn into dust and that's it? Well, to be honest, nobody really knows. No one has come back to tell us. I like to keep an open mind about all this. Look for these little signs. They might just give you some ideas or peace of mind, as that little bird did for me.

Forgiveness

You shall be, you shall be,
you shall be forgiven.—Ben Harper

I n life, many things can affect our emotions, and sometimes people's actions affect us in ways that cause hurt and pain. Relationships fail, money issues arise between couples, disagreements occur, the love flame burns out, passion fizzles, and general discontentment can take place. People leave each other for various reasons, some unexplainable. We fall in and out of love, one person seems to love the other more, clinging and attachment to one person can become uncomfortable for the other, and the breakdown of the relationship occurs—not to mention affairs, flirting, and just plain walking out the door, never to return.

When someone betrays us or leaves us, all our emotions erupt with guilt, fear, and loneliness. We cannot understand how our love life seemed to be going fine and then, *whammo*, we were knocked down and crying alone. It's hard to forgive when anger and crazy thoughts of revenge fill your mind and you wish bad things on your partner.

But there are things we cannot control. We cannot make someone love us or stay with us. People who cause us pain and anguish cannot be healthy for us in the long run. Sometimes we just have to move on and forgive that person and ourselves.

Of coure, that's easier to say than to do. Letting go and trusting that everything will work itself out may seem impossible at the time. It's very hard to let someone you love go, even when in your view that person has hurt you. You still crave and want to cling to that person, and that is mainly due to your ego, pride, and of course, fear.

Forgiveness is not easy. At times it is very painful, but if we look at it deeply, at the end of the day, there is no peace for us without forgiveness. It can take a strong person to say "I'm sorry," but it takes a stronger person to forgive. If you really want to feel love, you must try to learn to forgive.

Maybe you don't think some people deserve forgiveness, and I understand in certain situations—when a loved one has been murdered or cruelty and pain has been inflicted by undesirable humans—it is almost impossible to imagine forgiving someone like that. But your mind will never be at peace and pain will stay with you if you don't try to let go. Once you take those small steps forward, some of the anger and disappointment will fade.

Yes, at times I have found it very hard to forgive, but loving yourself and healing yourself will help in this process. A lot of times, we are seeking an apology, and we don't get it. Explanations as to why things happened the way they did—we don't get that either. Sometimes I guess we have to be okay without that "sorry" we don't get.

We have a choice every day to take whatever attitude we need to face the day. Try to start the day with the intention of being happy. When going through difficult or depressing times, attempt to be grateful. Get enough sleep, exercise, eat well, breathe deeply, and relax. Let the universe play its part. Let your amazing life take its course. Look after yourself.

If we keep dwelling on our past actions or thinking of somebody who has hurt us, it only keeps us in mental anguish. Timing is everything. If events are supposed to happen, they will, and for reasons we sometimes cannot explain. You have this one life. Believe in yourself; make yourself strong and proud.

No one can control you—only your thoughts. Change your thoughts if you have to. We cannot change the past and we cannot change the fact that some people will act in certain ways that we dislike. That's their path and journey; it does not have to be ours.

Forgive yourself. Forgive others. Move forward. Let go. Enjoy life's journey wherever it takes you. It does not matter if someone is a relative or a lover or a friend, removing toxic people from your life will relieve you of pain and suffering. If certain people disrespect you or your feelings and continue to treat you in a harmful way, they need to go.

Someday, you will forget the hurt if you let things unfold in time. Live the life you want. Love and forgive. All that matters is that you lived a good life. Move forward, be with people who support you, laugh, and try to forgive. As I have said before, it's a mystical journey we are on. Try to let it flow with as little drama as you can.

The One You Feed

An old Indian chief told his grandson, "My son, there is a battle between two wolves inside us all. One is evil. It is anger, jealousy, greed, resentment, inferiority, lies, and ego. The other is good. It is joy, peace, love, hope, humility, kindness, empathy, and truth.

The boy thought about what his grandfather had just explained about the battle of the two wolves inside us. He then asked, "Grandfather, which one wins?"

The old man quietly replied, "The one you feed."

—Unknown

M ost of us have a constant battle with our thoughts, thousands of times a day, ideas and emotions coming and going. Sometimes it feels like two voices in our heads fighting: Should I do this? Should I do that? We have to make decisions on everything in our daily lives.

The story above might just make you think a little about how powerful your mind and emotions are. Take time to read it over and over again. This can help during times of confusion and when your mind is restless. Be aware of which emotions you are feeding.

Nature

It's in the wind, it's in the trees,
Listen hard and you will see,
It's in the waves up from the sea.

—Xavier Rudd

I f you live in a fast-paced world of long days, skipped meals, and not enough sleep, one way to refresh yourself is to find nature. Most of us can find solace somewhere, whether it's a small park bench or the ocean shore, or even a walk out in the fresh air. Even if you live or work in the big city—the concrete jungle, as they call it—there is usually a way to escape the work environment for a few moments to find some peace and quiet.

Try to venture out from time to time to the ocean or mountains or parklands—whichever is close by—and be mindful of your surroundings. Smell the salt air and watch the waves rolling in. Listen to the sound of the birds, the wind, whatever is happening around you. Be at peace. Use all your senses, relax, and take it all in. Feel the grass beneath your feet, touch the sand, and feel the warmth of the sun on your face. Go out into a brisk winter day and feel the coolness of the wind and crispness in the air.

Wherever you are, lie on your back and look at the clouds or the stars. Be in the moment. Forget your worries for a short time. Don't be too concerned that they will still be there if you let your thoughts wander. We have so many opportunities around us to escape the rat race and our busy schedules, even if just to recharge our batteries for a short time.

Just be. Bring peace back to yourself, even if only for short bursts of time. Nature can rejuvenate your body and mind if you are willing to let go, relax, and be aware of your surroundings. Most times, Mother Nature comes to us for free. Embrace whatever she sends.

Travel

I'd fly above the trees,
Over the seas in all degrees, to anywhere I please.

—*Lenny Kravitz*

I f you get the chance to travel, go ahead and do it. Travel opens your mind to different cultures and traditions. Get out of your comfort zone and go explore. Talk to the local people, eat different foods, and experience a different way of life. This can be liberating; it can bring awareness that we are all the same—we are all human beings.

We may have different beliefs or lifestyles, but we share the common traits of trying to be happy and avoiding pain. Sometimes, visiting other countries can bring back your appreciation of what you have and how fortunate you are. It really can change your perspective on life and give you more compassion, gratitude, and respect for human behaviour, good or bad.

Not all of us have the opportunity or the finances to jump on an aircraft to exotic places. I totally understand this. But you can certainly tour your own city or even the suburbs instead. Pack a picnic basket and head north or south for a few hours in your car. Find a nice location and enjoy a new experience.

Sometimes we limit ourselves to our own little world. We may commute back and forth to work each day yet never get too far from home. We become comfortable and confined in our environment and familiar surroundings.

Checking out new places can be exciting and fun. Try it!

12

Change

We are biding our time for these myths to unwind.
These changes we will confront.

—Xavier Rudd

Have you ever noticed that life is constant changing? Nothing is permanent; in fact, everything is impermanent. We tend to crave for and cling to many things in our lives. Our desires consume us, and a lot of times we get frustrated and disappointed when we don't get what we want or someone leaves us. We tend to make a lot of "if only" or "what if" statements: *If only I had more money. If only I had a better job. What if I was to meet my perfect partner or to get big house? Then maybe I would be happy.*

If you look closely, all happiness is short-term, and change never stops. Of course, there is nothing wrong with acquiring nice and comfortable things (or people in some instances), more money, and more love, but we have to be a bit more mindful of the outcome. Everything comes and goes, and everything changes—even ourselves.

Most of the time, we resist change. We like to hold tight to our possessions, our partners, our money, our thoughts—just about everything. We grasp and cling, and when change takes place or we lose something, pain, fear, and insecurity become our friends.

I have read that this is like holding a hot coal in the palm of your hand. It hurts, but you don't want to let go because you're afraid of change. But when you do, the pain goes.

Impermanence is not all bad. Without it, we would never be able to grow. Change can bring maturity, wisdom, and awakening. As you become aware of this, you can appreciate your journey and what you have.

Again, be grateful; be content. Sometimes it's good to take a step back and see how change can affect us. Life is always changing—good times, bad times, unhappy times, happy times. It just keeps flowing, so go with it and enjoy the ride. No matter how down you are or how happy you feel, refer to this famous saying: "This too shall pass." The passage that follows kind of sums up this chapter.

Once the world was not here, now it's here,
and one day it won't be.
The seasons, they come and they
go, they come and they go.
Night turns into day, and day into night.
Even you, once you were not here, now you are here,
and one day you won't be here.
Your thoughts, they will come and go …
It's impermanent … everything is impermanent.

—Unknown

CHAPTER 13

Strange Little Moments

Please don't look my way when
you see me on the street.
We will still be strangers when we meet.

—The Smithereens

H ave you ever thought about some of the little unusual moments that occur in your life? For instance, you're going for a walk or out shopping, and you bump into someone you have not seen in years. You generally engage in small talk along the lines of, "Hey, it's been years!" "Wow, you look great!" "What have you been up to?" After a few uncomfortable moments, you go on your way and may never cross paths with that person again.

Just think, if you'd left your house five minutes earlier or later, this moment would never have taken place. So why did this happen at this time? Maybe you have been thinking of someone and then your phone rings or a text message comes through from that very person. Is this part of the puzzle of connection?

Sometimes we worry about going to an event, thinking we may cross paths with someone from our past who we do not wish to interact with for whatever reason. We worry for days, only to arrive and find that the person is not even there.

How many times do we make stories up in our minds that never happen? This occurs when we project our thoughts into the future. The mind is a very powerful tool that tricks us almost daily. Our stomachs churn, and we live in fear, wondering what someone else is doing or who they are with, or does this person like me or not? It goes on and on. It's endless.

Most times, the story you are telling yourself will not come to pass. All that thinking, stress, anxiety, and fear are for nothing. On the occasions when the story is true, you can then deal with it in the now, which is all we have.

Lots of little events occur in our lives that we don't pay too much attention to. Think of the times you have been on vacation—the build-up, planning, organizing, telling everybody how fantastic it will be. But when you get there, it's not what you imagined or not up to your expectations. This can happen. Yet we're constantly on our smartphones or devices, taking photos to show everybody back home how great it is and how lucky we are. We rush around trying to fit everything in, not taking time to enjoy the moment.

The days can drag on, and we wish we were home. Most people will tell you, "It was a great holiday, but I am so glad to be home." A few days later, we go back to our daily routine, like the holiday never happened.

Be aware of the strange little things we humans do. There are many. Maybe contemplate them a little and wonder why this is happening. Take time to be in the moment, the now, and enjoy. Think of the people you encounter or who are in your life—the ones who have come and gone or stayed.

Maybe the reason for our little moments will be explained when the puzzle of life is complete. Try not to judge people. You are on your path and so are they.

Everyone you meet is fighting a battle
you know nothing about. Be kind, always.

—Unknown

37

Thoughts

I'm wasting no more time, I'm wasting no more time.
I'm always gonna tell you what's on my mind.

—*The Cranberries*

Our thoughts come and go thousands of times a day. *Will I get out of bed? Will I have a good day? What will I have for lunch? Who will I meet today?* It just goes on and on, never stopping, thoughts, thoughts, thoughts.

Everyday life presents us with many options and choices. It's always your choice to manage how you feel and how you think. Happy thoughts uplift you; put negative thoughts out there, and that's you will get. More people will be drawn to your energy and outlook on life if you radiate a good mood.

Fearful and angry thoughts weaken you. Hate and fear eat away at you. You will never feel relaxed. You will be on edge and never at peace. Shame, guilt, and fear push you away from love, harmony, and a sense of well-being. Happy thoughts create good energy, and this can benefit your health and mind.

Oh, I know what you're saying—thinking happy thoughts is easier said than done. You are right, but at least we can try. That's a start.

Holding on to resentment will only weaken you. We tend to blame others for how we feel when in fact, it's just our thoughts. We cannot control other people's way of thinking. Try to shift your thoughts to love and forgiveness and wish others well on their journey.

You have a choice of what you let come into your mind. Hold onto the good and discard the bad. No one controls your thoughts. They are yours.

When we go into the past, we generally have regrets, resentment, or jealousy. We think the old days were so much better. Thinking of the future brings planning, fear, and of course, worry.

If you look at yourself right now, in most cases you are generally all right. Your heart is beating, amd you are breathing. I'm not saying everything is perfect or going your way, but if you have the basics of food, shelter, water, health, and a sound mind, you should be okay.

When a crisis strikes, your body may be in pain and your mind filled with negative emotions, but try to ride out the storm. Storms always pass. Try to forgive yourself or someone who has rejected you or has used or abused you. Look after yourself and your health. Get enough sleep. Eat well, exercise, and drink plenty of water. Seek out your friends for support when trouble arises. Take time for yourself. It may seem like heavy clouds are hanging over your head, but they will lift, and the sun will shine on you once again.

Being attached to possessions and people can bring us discomfort. Often we have closed minds. Try to open your heart and mind to different views. Listen, take in information, and decide for yourself.

Many things and events affect our thoughts. Sometimes we may think we need revenge for the pain and heartache someone has caused us, but again, these are only thoughts. Try to let events unfold in their own way. Breathe and find peace with your thoughts. Try not to decide or speak before you settle your mind. Take time with this. It can bring better results.

It's your life and your choice how you think. Sometimes it's hard being aware of what's happening right now. We may wish circumstances and people were different. It's difficult to deal with unpleasant feelings and pain. We think it's going to be like this for a long time, but it won't.

It's good to approach each day with an open heart and no judgement. Try to be grateful for good things and accept that not everything will go your way. Make peace with your thoughts and yourself.

Quiet Time

And whispered in the sounds of silence.

—*Paul Simon*

We live in a very fast-paced world that is full of consumerism. It seems we are always on the go. We have work, parenting, sports, and shopping to attend to, as well as our daily chores. How do we fit all this in? Just being attached to our technological devices eats away many of our waking hours. How often do we say, "There are never enough hours in the day." Taking time out each day to be still and quiet is not as simple as it seems.

When I ask most people if they take time out, the general response is, "I don't have time." I often reply, "Do you have time to go to the bathroom?" The answer, of course, is yes.

"Do you drive or commute to work?" Yes.

"Do you lay on the couch and watch TV?" Yes.

"Do you spend hours on your phone checking and updating your profile?" Yes.

If you have time to do these things, you have time to calm your mind. I am not suggesting that you have to sit on a mountain and meditate for years, or sit in church and pray for hours, but if you can find time to relax—to still your mind—you may be able to calm some of your mental anguish. Breaking old habits or trying a new way can result in a calmer you.

Try this exercise: Stay still, and breathe in and out easily. Try not to force the breath. You will feel your mind drift off to the past or the future. Try to relax into the present moment. When your mind wanders, just come back to your breath. Feel it coming in and out. Acknowledge your thoughts, and then let them come and go. Doing this for a few minutes a day can bring amazing results.

Happiness

If it makes you happy, it can't be that bad.
If it makes you happy,
Then why the hell are you so sad?

—*Sheryl Crow*

M aybe the purpose of life is to be happy. How do you find happiness? That is the question.

In our daily life, we often get lost in our thoughts—thinking of the past and sometimes fearing the future. Happiness, it seems, can be found in the now. Yet often, we get lost in the pursuit of material things or having people around us to fill our boredom. Most times we are not content; we want more and more. Once we get a house, we want a bigger one. The new job brings more stress. More money only leaves us wanting more.

All the things we acquire are very nice, and there is nothing wrong with having these in our lives, but we must remember that they only bring short-term happiness. The new car becomes old, the iPhone becomes outdated, your partner becomes boring. You know how it goes. We are always searching for the next new thing. Social media and advertising play a large role in this, as we have quick access to almost everything and can discard things and people too easily.

It has to begin with you. Love yourself and then try to help others. This could be the first step.

Instead, we just seem to consume more and more. We tend to think of ourselves and our immediate needs and desires. Not having what we think we are entitled to can be our main concern, the main focus of unhappiness and frustration. We develop a *me, me, me* attitude, always thinking *if only I had this or that, then I could be really happy.* Sometimes we just need to be happy with what we have or set goals to obtain things without needing immediate results.

Most of us living in the Western world have good lives. What do we really want out of our lives? To work longer? To gain more possessions? To spend more time at the office or on the job? To make more money to pay for everything to keep up our so-called lifestyle? Maybe we just need a bit more balance.

Sure, having money makes life a little easier, but for some reason we always find discontentment no matter what occurs. I doubt you will hear anyone say, "I wish I worked more." Yes, of course, we need to work to provide for our families and ourselves. This is responsible and keeps societies functioning. Again, though, balance seems to be the key—combining work and leisure. Maybe work to live instead of living to work.

Happiness is a very strong desire, and at the end of the day, it comes down to choices. Look at a wave in the ocean. When it rises high, imagine yourself on top. This is the highest feeling of happiness. We wish the feeling would stay like this, but as we all know, the wave comes crashing down and sadness occurs. But do not fear—the wave rises again. It's a cycle that continues throughout our lives. Enjoy the happy moment while it lasts and acknowledge the sad times when they hit. Be aware that no one escapes these feelings.

We tend to blame everyone and everything for our state of mind, when in fact it is our responsibility to select our own thoughts. When we feel happy, people like to be around us. We can be in the position to help others when we are happy. When helping others, we are not thinking of ourselves all the time.

Most times, things do not need to be different in our lives for us to seek happiness. Our unhappiness comes from our thoughts. The desire to be happy takes practice, and in some cases it requires change. We have looked at gratefulness and contentment throughout this book. Tapping into these two emotions and feelings can be a great start to feeling happy and at ease with yourself.

Most happy people are uplifting, caring, compassionate, and vibrant. They are a pleasure to be around. Unhappy people think life is always difficult and depressing. Of course, this affects the people around them.

Practice making a choice each day when awakening. Look forward to seeing how your day unfolds. Be positive and energetic, and embrace what's ahead. Smile a bit more. Breathe deep and help others. Remember, it's a new day every day— one you will never have again. It's up to you to make the most of it. Good luck!

Be true to yourself. Be grateful and content. Love more, and most of all, enjoy your summers.

Everybody wants to live, how they want to live,
and everybody wants to love, who they want to love,
and everybody wants to be closer to free.

—*The BoDeans*

Quotes

To further your reflection, I've gathered more of my favorite quotes about life and share them here with some of my own thoughts on these life-impacting subjects.

Impermanence

*Everything in life is temporary, so if things
are going good, enjoy it, because it won't last
forever, and if things are going bad, don't worry,
it can't last forever either.—Unknown*

If you think about impermanence, you will come to see that it is the essence of life. Everything is constantly changing—nothing stays the same. Understanding that everything and everybody comes and goes can make us look at the world and people from a different perspective. It's not always a negative thing. We need to change to grow and to see things as they actually are.

Change can hurt, change can bring fear, change can renew you. The world keeps spinning around, and we keep moving forward, constantly changing. Most times we don't notice moment-to-moment change, but everything is changing, even you, growing from baby to adult to old age. When we start to recognize impermanence, we can fully understand our life experiences and let go of fears, regrets, and day-to-day disappointments.

Because nothing is permanent and everything is possible, no two days are ever the same. Each will never happen again. When we want things to stay the same, that's when we suffer. We cling and hold on to the things in our lives, but eventually everything goes. It sounds a little depressing, I know, but it's the truth—it's reality. Embrace it, and you will want to live your life in a different manner. Impermanence teaches us what we already know but do not want to examine most times: time passes no matter what happens in our lives.

Sometimes we have to make shifts in life to help us move forward. If you start to accept change, it can become your greatest teacher. All of us, at whatever stage we have reached in our lives, will experience impermanence. It is what it is. We do not have to fear it. It can bring peace.

Look around you, and you'll see things changing. Look in the mirror, and you'll see yourself changing. You are not the same person you were yesterday. Don't be complacent; if there are things you want to do, don't put them off. Time moves quickly. Don't take your days for granted. We can either resist change and be angry or frustrated, or we can accept that life is unpredictable and live it as best we can.

Nobody lives forever, nothing stands the test of time.
Oh you heard them say "never say never,"
But it's always best to keep it in mind.

—Steve Earle

Strength

Sometimes walking away has nothing to do with
weakness and everything to do with strength.
We walk away not because we want others
to realize our worth and value, but because
we finally reach our own.—Unknown

Sometimes in this beautiful but overwhelming world we live in, we need to be strong. We are tested in our relationships, in our jobs, and in the course of general survival. Stay positive and realize your value to society. Understand who you are. Strive for inner strength, not only for you but for others.

Life can throw many things at us to test us, to weaken us. Sometimes the behaviour of others can give us grief or make us feel uneasy. Don't let this happen; be strong. When bad things happen, don't let them affect you—let them strengthen you. You have to be strong enough to live your life the way you wish.

Showing emotion is a sign of strength; don't be afraid of it. You also have to be strong enough to sometimes let go. Some people may like to see you fall. Stand your ground, smile, and stay strong.

Give me strength to carry on,
Give me strength I must feel strong,
Give me strength to carry on,
Feels like all my hope is gone.

—Howard Jones

Insecurities

Confidence is silent,
insecurities are loud.

—Unknown

Build your confidence. Stand and walk tall. There's no need to be arrogant or cocky, just carry confidence in everything you do to know your goals and fulfil your dreams. Insecurities are loud—a weakness, a touch of fear. Be confident, lose the insecurities, and move through life in the direction you desire.

Insecurities can make us feel weak, and a lot of times we seek approval and acceptance. Insecurity can destroy friendships, relationships, and work opportunities. Your confidence suffers as you fear that you are not good enough. Insecurity can stop you from trying new things.

Stop comparing yourself to other people—you are you. Believe in yourself and be happy with yourself. Say what you feel; stop worrying about what others think. Insecurity can destroy you. Don't let that happen. Love yourself.

I believe we can change anything.
I believe we can rise above this
I believe there's a reason for everything.

—Joe Satriani

Speech

Take care of your thoughts when alone,
And take care of your words when you are with people.

—Unknown

Most times we speak before we think. Choose your words wisely; once spoken, they can never be taken back. We seem to always want to voice our opinion but not listen to the person talking—cutting people mid-sentence, finishing their story, or blurting out our own.

Listen carefully, speak in a controlled manner, and choose your words appropriately. Words are powerful. Harsh words can hurt a person. Think before you speak, because you can never get those words back. Sometimes it's better to be silent.

Often, when we're angry, we don't really mean what we say. Before this occurs, step aside and cool down a bit. Let your emotions be at ease, and then think about what you want to say. If you keep hearing negative speech or harsh words from people, you may have to ask yourself why you keep allowing this.

There comes a time to release negative people and actions from your life. Most of us have been hurt by words, so think about your talk and how it can affect others. Be careful with your speech when emotional or in different moods. Emotions and moods change quickly, but it's hard to take back your words.

Don't speak
I know what you're saying
So please stop explaining
Don't tell me cause it hurts.

—No Doubt

Feeling Uneasy

If you are feeling uneasy about something or someone,
Always remember that time discovers the truth.

—Unknown

We all at times get that uneasy feeling about something or someone. We feel it in our stomachs, and it stays in our minds. It keeps us awake and on edge. Anxiety and being restless about our lives can make us feel uneasy. The feeling is constantly with us; we're dissatisfied about our day-to-day life.

We don't know what we want. Life becomes boring; we just go through the motions. Constant thoughts about someone who maybe has left us or hurt us can bring uneasiness. We blame ourselves for others' behaviour or put ourselves down and feel guilty, even though we have done nothing wrong. Be patient. The truth always wins.

That's why I'm easy. I'm easy like Sunday morning.

—*Faith No More*

Jealousy

A sign of insecurity,
A sign of weakness,
A sign of obsession.

—*Unknown*

Jealousy can represent a lack of self-confidence or a burning feeling of not being wanted—or of wanting what other people seem to have. If people are busy discussing your life, they are probably jealous or not happy with their own. Jealousy is a fear of comparison. Let it go.

Jealousy often rears its ugly head when love is involved. It kicks in when you think you are unwanted or not loved anymore, or when a person who you think loves you prefers somebody else. Jealousy springs from insecurity. If you are confident person, this should not affect you. Don't let the feeling of being unwanted or pushed aside eat away at you.

We always think the other person who has left us is happy and having a great life. In a lot of cases, this is not true. Stop worrying about what others are doing. Be self-confident, move on, find your freedom, and find your love.

I was feeling insecure,
you might not want me anymore.
I was shivering inside,
I was shivering inside.

—John Lennon

Gossip

A lot of problems in the world would
disappear if we would talk to each other
instead of about each other.—Unknown

My only advice on this one is to try to avoid gossip. It makes some people feel better about themselves, especially if you agree with them; it gives them a sense of power. Most people who gossip are hiding their own insecurities and fears and know their own lives are not what they expected, or they are trapped in boredom. Some people are quick to believe stories they hear about good people.

You'll hear it in your workplace—it's almost impossible to avoid it. You'll hear it from your family and friends—it's ongoing. We all have a tendency to talk about others and their downfalls. Stop judging people to make yourself feel better. Gossip is just a tool to distract people who have nothing better to do. If there is gossip going on around you, stay out of it. What you say is a reflection on you.

People who gossip *to* you will almost definitely gossip *about* you, so beware. It's hard not to take things too personally when we hear gossip about ourselves, but again, it's generally a reflection on them, not you. When people talk behind your back, they generally have poor self-esteem and are trying to build themselves up. It always comes back to them. Usually, they have issues in their own lives that they are not acknowledging.

So maybe next time, before you speak about others when they are not present, ask yourself why. Is it helpful? Is it harmful? Is it really necessary? Remember: gossip is a sign of immaturity, and it always comes back at you.

I heard it on the grapevine
was just about to lose my mind
Oh, I'm just about to lose my mind.

—*Creedence Clearwater Revival*

Music

Music speaks what cannot be expressed,
soothes the mind and gives it rest,
heals the heart and makes it whole,
flows from heaven to the soul.

—*Unknown*

Music is a universal language. It brings joy and connection to so many people. Use it for relaxation and to escape from reality for a while. Whether shared, sung along too, or yelled at the top of your lungs, it can give you a feeling of joy and bliss.

Broaden your horizons and explore different types of music. You may surprise yourself and your ears. Music can feed our emotions and help us escape from reality. It speaks to us in ways that move us.

Music can help us in many ways. It eases our worries for a time and blocks out the noisy world. It brings a smile to your face or makes you cry with the sadness of the lyrics. The power of music should not be underestimated—it can change your mood and your way of thinking. It can take you back or inspire you. It's always there for you.

Everybody deserves music, sweet music.

—Michael Franti

People

Life does not always introduce you to people you want to meet. Sometimes life puts you in touch with the people you need to meet to help you, to leave you, to love you, and to gradually strengthen you into the person you were meant to become.—Unknown

With all the billions of people in the world, we have different cultures, religions, points of view, and unusual thought patterns. What binds us is that we all want happiness and to avoid pain. In the end, we are all the same.

People come and go in our lives, and some stay. Remember, we all have the same blood, same emotions, and same fears. We are all trying to do our best and find our way. We all make mistakes, and we all need love. Don't judge people because they look or talk differently. We are all connected in some way.

We can be strange creatures at times. We have the highest brain function of anything on this planet, but we can destroy things for our own short-term needs, and we can cause wars with our ideals and greediness. We can also create and make amazing things, help others, and live wonderful lives.

Appreciate good people—they are hard to find. The best people are those who love you for simply being you. Love them back.

Keep things simple. Keep your attitude positive, and try to maintain a balanced life. Help others, and happiness will be yours.

Come on people now, smile on your brother,
everybody get together, try and love
one another right now.

—*The Youngbloods*

Hurt

Nobody can make you suffer;
All they can do is impinge upon your senses.
They can make you see certain things,
They can make you hear certain things,
They can make you smell, taste, feel, or
possibly make you think certain things,
But they can't make you react to
those things in a certain way.
No one can hurt you.

—*Unknown*

Hurt can come to us in many ways. Pain can be inflicted on our bodies. People's attitudes and words can hurt us. Behaviour can hurt, and we can be emotionally hurt. Someone can make us feel special one minute and unwanted the next.

At some point, you will realize that you have done too much for someone or something. Sometimes you have to stop and walk away. We often put our expectations up high only to be disappointed or hurt by the actions of others, but it all comes down to you. Your thoughts are yours and yours alone.

People may not always perceive you the way you want them to. You do not have power over their actions, and you may never understand them. Others have their thoughts and reasons, and so do you. There are situations that you cannot change, but the hurt will fade; give it time.

There will always be someone who hurts you, but you have to keep trusting. Just be more careful who you trust. Let things unfold, and one day, you will forget the hurt.

My empire of dirt
I will let you down
I will make you hurt.

—Nine Inch Nails

Past

The past should be left in the past,
Otherwise it can destroy your future.
Live life for what tomorrow has to offer,
Not for what yesterday has taken away.

—Unknown

Sometimes things don't turn out the way we wished. The past is over, and we are constantly changing and growing. We find it hard to be happy sometimes, because we always think the past was better. But the future can be so much better than the past.

Learn from the past; it can give you wisdom. What is meant to come your way will come your way. Relax and let things be. If you think about it, the only important thing is living now, not in the past. Yesterday is gone.

You cannot erase past memories, but you don't always have to dwell on them. The only thing to do is accept them. It can be nice at times to drift back into the past for some great memories of good times or remembering loved ones who have left this earth, but in most cases, it's not so good to keep going back over things.

Don't be too concerned about yesterday. Think of the opportunities tomorrow can bring. We all make mistakes. We have all made wrong decisions that have shaped who we are today. Don't let the past have power over you or control you; don't let it ruin your happiness.

Remember, if your past was very hard or you have regrets, tomorrow is a new beginning—a new start. It's your choice: stay stuck in the past or live in the now. Who knows what the future will bring?

It'll be better than before
Yesterday's gone, yesterday's gone.

—Fleetwood Mac

Food

Food is essential to life. Therefore,
make it good.—Unknown

We all need food; we all love food. It's fuel for our bodies. You will see all sorts of diets and fads in the media telling you what's good and what's bad for you. It can all become very confusing.

It always seems like the food that tastes the worst is the best for us. Our taste buds seem to love sweet, sugary things. Enjoy them every now and then. I think it all comes down to balance. Fast food is so easy and accessible to us, but let's limit it a bit or, if possible, cut it out for good. Your body will get used to not having it.

It all comes down to choice. Try thinking before you eat. Moderation is the key. Most of us have access to fresh produce and clean water. Once you make the lifestyle change, it's hard to go back to fatty, sweet, unhealthy foods. Give it a try. You'll find you have more energy and vitality to enjoy everything in life.

I don't care if you're full, just eat it, eat it, eat it, eat it,
open up your mouth and feed it.

—*Weird Al Yankovic*

Smile

Let your smile change the world,
but don't let the world change your smile.

—*Unknown*

There really is a lot to smile about. Just change your thoughts and actions. Smile at others, and you will normally get a smile back. A smile can help you face every moment, hiding the pain or showing your joy. When you feel sad or depressed, these emotions may try to steal your smile.

Be conscious of how you present yourself. A smile can be very welcoming and put people at ease. Smiling brings warmth and love and can be infectious. Even little things in life can make you smile—seeing someone you love, being excited about going somewhere, feeling grateful. Little smiles come to us on many occasions.

Try smiling more. Don't let negativity or the drama in your life drag you down. A smile speaks all languages.

God gave you style and gave you grace
and put a smile on your face.

—Coldplay

Let Go

At some point you have to realize that some people can stay in your heart, but not in your life.—Unknown

Wade McGauley

It's sometimes very hard to find the courage to let go of what you can't change. Letting go doesn't mean you have to stop loving or caring. Sometimes we have to understand that not all people should stay in our lives. We have to stop trying to justify why we hold onto toxic people and circumstances. Best to move on and learn some lessons—not an easy task sometimes, but it may bring you peace.

Love comes and goes, sometimes
decades, sometimes months.

—Xavier Rudd

Gratitude

No regrets, just lessons.
No worries, just acceptance.
No expectations, just gratitude.
Life is short.

—Unknown

We never seem to be content—always wanting more, feeling lost, and wishing and hoping for better things and better times. Stop complaining so much. If you could only play things back at the end of the day and listen to speech and thoughts, you will see how much negative energy you are putting out. You have a precious human life; your heart is beating, and you are breathing. Give thanks, and you will end up with more. What you put out to the universe, you will get back. Gratitude is the best attitude.

One life you got to do what you should.
One life, with each other.

—U2

Love

Don't settle for anybody
just so you can have somebody.—Unknown

Being in love is the romantic part: the laughs, conversations, togetherness, and feeling of connection. It's beautiful, and a very hard feeling to describe. It's good to be in love. But we all know it can change very quickly. Love fades, arguments take place, and sadness and dissatisfaction arise.

There are many different levels of love, and we love in many ways. We love our partners, our family, our friends, our pets, our food, and so on. Love is born into us. Being nurtured as a baby is unconditional love. It just seems to get a bit complicated after that. We start our search, and our egos confuse us. Try to love yourself first, and the rest will follow.

Remember that love does not have to be perfect. It just has to be true. Great love can change your life, for better or worse.

My legs start to tremble, my knees start to shake,
my mind wants to crumble, my heart wants to break,
I nearly lost control, till I met you.

—Jason and the Scorchers

Mindfulness

You can never be happy if you're trapped in
the past and fearful of the future. Living in the
present is the only way to be happy.—Unknown

Be mindful of what is happening around you. If you are feeling depressed, it's usually because you are living in the past or thinking about yourself. Concentrate on whatever you are doing in the now. Thinking too far ahead to the future can bring anxiety. Being mindful of the present is the key. Sometimes, just take a moment and tell yourself that you are who, what, and where you are supposed to be.

Be mindful in everything you do. Think about how you start to your day. This is when our minds are most projected into the future. You already know what you have to do and where to be, so slow your thoughts and enjoy everything, from waking up to showering, drinking coffee, driving your car to work, and so on.

Usually it's all a rush, and we can't even remember arriving at our destination. We are not mindful. Instead, take a look around at the sky, the flowers, and whatever is in your environment. Look at life happening right in front of you. Each moment that passes by will never be repeated the exact same way. Take time out to appreciate things and people. Try not to be late for work, though, okay?

This life, well, it's slipping right through your hands.
These days never turned out nothing like I had planned.
Control, well, it's slipping right through my hands.

—*Powderfinger*

Overthinking

Overthinking is the biggest cause of our unhappiness.
Keep yourself occupied. Keep your mind off things
that don't help you. Think positively.—*Unknown*

We have a tendency to imagine what should have been or what could have been. We sometimes make the simplest things into big problems. We make a lot of stories and scenarios up in our head. We overthink.

It can get to a stage where we stop doing what we should be doing because we're worried about the outcome. We create our own problems and dwell on them. Take time out, think less sometimes, and do things you love. Breathe, and you will see things work out the way they are supposed to.

Your thoughts are yours; no one controls them. If you don't like them, you have the ability to change them. Our minds are jumping from one thing to another most times, making us unsettled and disrupting pleasure or sleep. Some things we just cannot control. Let them unfold. Think about all the times you worried or overthought things and they never turned out the way you thought. Things you worried about a year ago, a month ago, even weeks ago, somehow don't seem important anymore.

So calm your mind and let life unfold. If you want to change things, take action. If events or things are uncontrollable, let them be. What else can we do?

I was thinking, overthinking
Cause there's just too many scenarios.

—Relient K

Good-bye

We start with a simple hello, but end with a complicated good-bye.—Unknown

Good-byes can be temporary or final. Throughout our day, we meet people with a hello, and at the end of the interaction we say good-bye. Good-byes in our love life can be sad and devastating. Some good-byes are never experienced; people just walk in and out of each other's lives.

Good-byes that go unsaid can be painful. When things get tough between people, sometimes they feel it's better to think the other person doesn't exist and just walk away—no good-bye. This can break your heart and disturb your mind, but there's not much you can do other than try to find forgiveness.

Most good-byes still mean, "I will see you again," but there are times when you know it's time to say good-bye for good. Communication is lost, we fall out of love, or we need a fresh start. It's time to move on.

Most Novembers, I break down and cry,
But I can't remember if we said good-bye.

—Steve Earle

Yes or No

The magic moment is that in which a yes or a no
may change the whole of our existence.—Unknown

All your decisions come down to a yes or a no. Your whole life consists of this; a spur-of-the-moment decision can affect you or many people in your life. Everything we do, everything we want—it's hard to master these two words, yes or no.

Sometimes we say yes to please people or to feel wanted, but if things don't feel right or people are hurting you, learn to say no. A lot of mistakes we make in life occur when we wanted to say no but ended up saying yes. Try not to keep saying yes to please people or to make certain things easier.

It can be difficult to say no when you really mean yes or the other way around. Think before you answer. There's no such thing as maybe. *Yes* or *no* changes your life for better or worse. Select wisely.

It seems to me that maybe, it pretty
much always means no.
So don't tell me, you might just let it go.

—Jack Johnson

Reality

There are things that we don't want to
happen but have to accept; things we
don't want to know but have to learn;
and people we can't live without but have
to let go.—Unknown

Most people only see what they want to see. We often live in dream world. Facing reality can be hard, but it's also liberating. Face some of your fears and learn the truth.

Reality can be frightening. Most times, we like to escape into our fantasies and refuse to acknowledge what's really happening in our lives and the world. It's easier sometimes not to face reality. We fear the unknown; life can be difficult, and we are constantly changing.

The world is a beautiful place, but it can also be fraught with danger and sadness. Open your eyes and accept what is. Be thankful you are here and on your journey. Face the truth, look at reality, and escape to fantasy only when needed. Be a realist.

In the real world, there are things that we can't change
And endings come to us in ways we can't rearrange.

—Roy Orbison

Lies

The truth doesn't cost anything,
but a lie could cost you everything.—Unknown

Pay less attention to what people say and more attention to what they do. Actions show truth. Liars can fool most people most of the times, but try to stay honest. A lot of liars think they are telling the truth, Once someone starts lying, it's very hard for people to trust that individual. It will eventually catch up with him or her.

It does not matter how big or small they are—lies are lies, and lies can destroy people. When liars' behaviour becomes questionable, they lie to get their way or to manipulate or to gain a sense of power and control. It becomes a habit for them, and it gets easier for them to do it if they are not caught. They often believe their own lies, and they rarely feel bad or show remorse.

Try to avoid these people. They are not trustworthy, and they will generally continue these actions with whoever they encounter. Once caught, they will move on to another victim. You do not need them in your life. If someone puts trust in you, never lie to that person. It's very simple.

I can see right through that thin disguise.
Can't you tell, I can tell when you're telling white lies.

—Jason and the Scorchers

Stress

Stop focusing on how stressed you are.
Remember how blessed you are.
It could be worse.

—Unknown

What is stress? People use this word all the time, but how do we define it? Is it a combination of things not going right in your life? Not getting what you want or think you deserve?

We worry and wonder. Maybe we should just let things work out the way they are meant to be and keep moving forward. We stress when we think life is being unkind to us and worrying about what we think might happen.

The best way to counteract stress is to change your thoughts. Keep busy. Do not sit around wallowing in self-pity, but put your energies into something positive. It's only your response to stress that affects you.

Stress is hard to avoid with so much going on in our lives. We all, at times, will feel stressed. If it gets to be too much, talk about it with someone or focus on what you can control. We tend to put ourselves under pressure, and that causes stress. Blaming things and outside influences won't help either.

Remember, you can't always have what you want. You must try to stop making up stories in your head. Everything unfolds the way it is supposed to.

It's the sweet things only time will bring
that arrive like a blessing in disguise.

—Bryan Adams

Age

Do not regret growing old.
It's a privilege denied to many.—Unknown

Aging comes to us all. Nothing can stop this. Each year you can only live once. Don't dwell on it. Your body will change; accept this. Embrace your age. Live in the now, and gain some wisdom.

Old man take a look at my life,
I'm a lot like you were.—Neil Young

Time

Three things you cannot recover in life:
The word after it's said;
The moment after it's missed;
And time after it's gone.

—Unknown

Time is very valuable. You can't buy time. Stop complaining about yesterday; it's gone. Stop saying, "I have plenty of time"; you don't. If you waste your time, you are wasting your life. Time creeps up on us slowly, and the years pass.

We worry so much, we stress, we get anxious—but in time, all these issues are dissolved. Find time to do what you love. Find your purpose, and give your time to others in need. Enjoy every minute you have. The clock is ticking.

If I could stop my mind from wondering
What I left behind
And from worrying about this wasted time.

—The Eagles

Communication

Without communication, there is no relationship.
Without respect, there is no love.
Without trust, there is no reason to continue.

—Unknown

Have we lost the art of communication? Too much technology, you say. Relationships are built and held on communication. We must learn how to communicate. We must listen to understand, not just to reply.

Communication is the key to any relationship. The passion dies down, the excitement fades, annoying habits arise, and trouble begins. The daily grind of paying the bills, keeping a household, and consuming many products pulls relationships into reality. Good solid relationships must have good communication. Instead of fighting or arguing, try expressing your opinion in a calm way.

We all have different views. We do not have to agree on everything, but we do have to be able to discuss anything. We need to listen more without always interrupting and trying to get our own point of view across. Communicate clearly with your friends, family, and others. Think before you speak.

Communication can keep relationships on track and strengthen them. Listen and communicate. Be open, and make your communication two-way.

Communication, say the words,
are you there, can I be heard?—Janet Jackson

Anger

Anger doesn't solve anything.
It builds nothing,
But it can destroy everything.

—Unknown

Anger is a very strong emotion, often bubbling away inside us and then rising to the top. When you speak in anger, you may regret it.

Lots of things can anger us: traffic jams, irritating people, the weather, not getting what we want. Minor and major issues can bring on anger. Anger is often a sign of hidden emotional problems for the individual. Fear and sadness are the most common. When people get angry at you, it's usually their hidden truths that arise. That person is usually holding a lot of pain.

If on occasion you do get angry—and we all do—try to walk away, take a deep breath, and calm down. Acknowledge your feelings and emotions. Tap into your anger to find the real reason you are acting this way, and then work on fixing it.

Try to hold your tongue when anger arises, or go somewhere alone and scream it out. If you speak, you may regret it. Anger really does not solve anything, and in fact the only person you are hurting is yourself.

Getting angry at people you think should change is not a good idea either. We are all on different paths. Compromising with someone is different from trying to change them. You do not always have to reply with anger if you are not getting your way.

Nobody can make you angry. It is your decision to respond that way.

My soul slides away,
But don't look back in anger,
But don't look back in anger, I heard you say.

—Oasis

Be Aware

Not everybody will appreciate what you do for them.
You have to figure out who's worth your kindness
And who's taking advantage.—Unknown

Be aware of how you live your life; it goes quick. Be aware of people who use you or attack your self-esteem. Be aware of your breathing. Be aware that everything changes. Time heals everything.

No one is in charge of your happiness. There is no place in your life for toxic people who use and abuse you. Surround yourself with positive people. Not everybody will appreciate you, so find the ones who deserve your love and kindness.

Brought you around and you just brought me down.

—Plain White T's

Anxiety

Don't let your difficulties fill you with anxiety,
After all, it is only in the darkest nights
that stars shine more brightly.

—Unknown

Stress and fear usually bring on feelings of anxiety. Think about who cares about you or who is using you. Notice feelings of not being good enough or happy, of wanting to be liked or attention-seeking. Needing the approval from others and overthinking can fill us with anxiety.

There are many things that cause this, but mainly our thoughts and fears. A lot of the time, we get anxious about things we cannot control. That's when anxiety eats away at our hearts and minds. Anxiety is not nice; it can stop you from enjoying your life. Anxiety is about control, but being anxious about the future or its outcome will not change anything.

It's hard to relax sometimes. Find things you like doing; be with people who support you and who you trust. Understand that you can't control everything; just let it unfold. Once again—try to relax into the now.

Look at the stars, look how they shine for you
and all the things that you do.

—Coldplay

Healing

Rejection doesn't hurt, expectation does.
Forgetfulness doesn't heal, forgiveness does.

Healing is both mental and physical. Both can take time. When your body becomes sick, you need to seek help, advice, and care. Take time out to recover, and be kind to yourself. In your emotional state, you need to let go of things you can't control. This will bring peace.

Try to keep away from drama and from toxic, negative people. Learn to heal, learn to forgive, and learn to love.

So you've been broken and you've been hurt,
Show me somebody who ain't.

—Bruce Springsteen

Trust

Let go of the need to control the outcome.
Trust the outcome,
Trust the process,
Trust your intuition,
Trust yourself.

—Unknown

Trust, it is said, is the foundation that holds relationships. Trust is gained. You have to trust the person you love. Without trust, there is nothing.

It's hard to recover trust after it's lost. Actions speak louder than words, they say. Your gut feelings are usually right. Learning to trust can be difficult. Once a promise is broken, a "sorry" can be worthless.

I know I really, really want to trust you.

—Rob Thomas

Worry

Worry does not take away tomorrow's troubles,
It takes away today's peace.—Unknown

Why do we worry so much? Things we worried about weeks, months, or even years ago don't seem relevant or important as time goes by. Maybe we should get excited about what's ahead and what can go right instead of focusing on the negative. If you really think about it, most things we worry about never happen. Thinking and worrying about everything will never change the outcome.

Don't worry about a thing
Cause every little thing gonna be all right.

—Bob Marley

Confidence

Stop hating yourself for everything you are not.
Start loving yourself for everything you are.

—Unknown

There is a difference between being confident and being arrogant or rude. It's about being positive in who you are and where you are headed. See good in every situation; stop worrying about what others think. Be self-confident. Stop trying to compare yourself to others.

You are you. Accept your strengths and weaknesses. Believe in yourself.

Just do your best, do everything you can,
And don't worry about what the
bitter hearts are gonna say.

—*Jimmy Eat World*

Dreams

A good life is when you assume nothing.
Do more, need less, smile often, dream big.
Laugh a lot and realize how blessed
you are for what you have.

—*Unknown*

Sometimes we don't do or achieve the things we want to do. We just dream. We can shake ourselves from this complacent state and make our dreams come true. It takes courage, but in most cases if you can dream it, you can do it. The only time it's impossible is in your mind.

Most of us are walking around in a dreamlike state. We need to awaken. Chase your dreams if you desire. You need to start to achieve them.

Oh that's what dreams are made of.
Oh baby, we belong in a world that must be strong.
Oh that's what dreams are made of.

—Van Halen

Your Actions

Everything you do is based on the choices
you make. It's not your parents, your past
relationships, your job, the economy, the weather,
an argument, or your age that's to blame. You
and only you are responsible for every decision
and choice you make, period.—Unknown

Many times we do not take responsibility for our own actions. We are always blaming someone else for the situation we are in. We have to stop making excuses and make changes. No matter how you are feeling, you are responsible for how you act.

Your actions and speech can affect many people. Be wise with them. It's always about you.

And who to blame, you to blame,
Me to blame
For the pain and it poured every time it rained.
Let's play the blame game.

—Kanye West

Compassion

Sometimes what a person needs is not a brilliant mind that speaks, but a patient heart that listens.—Unknown

As human beings, we will all experience pain and suffering at some stage. Mental anguish or body pain will come for all of us. When someone comes to you with these issues, try to show compassion. Do not interrupt or finish their sentences or tell your story. It's about them, remember, not you. Listen with intent. We all need to do this. It's compassionate.

Love and compassion, love and compassion,
Give it to you,
Give it to me.

—Hall and Oates

Loss

Be strong enough. Let go and be patient enough
to wait for what you deserve.—Unknown

In life, we will eventually lose everything. On the way through your journey, loss will come at many different times. Lovers leave, friends and family die, money goes, our looks fade, and health declines. We can lose our keys or even our minds.

If you can remember that everything comes and goes, and take the good with the bad, you will be okay. What else can we do?

I'm broken down like a train wreck.
Well it's over I know but I can't let go.

—Lucinda Williams

Sad

Everybody wants happiness, nobody
wants pain, but you can't have a rainbow
without a little rain.—Unknown

Sadness can hit us at any time. We drift in and out of sadness. Life situations make us sad. People make us sad. We make ourselves sad.

Acknowledge your sad feelings. Ask yourself why you feel this way. Let the emotion stay with you, and then try to let it go. Focus on good thoughts, breathe, and relax. Everything will be okay.

It's hard to believe that there's nobody out there.
It's hard to believe that I'm all alone.

—*Red Hot Chili Peppers*

Self-Love

Focus on loving yourself instead of loving the
idea of other people loving you.—*Unknown*

Lots of people have this issue of loving themselves. It's a hard concept for some to take on. It's all about inner peace and being proud of who you are and where you are going.

Stop beating yourself up about your insecurities and flaws. We all have them. Accept them or change them. We are all individuals, not one and the same. Be kind to yourself. Love yourself.

You live, you learn, you love, you learn,
You cry, you learn,
You bleed, you learn
You scream, you learn.

—Alanis Morisette

Pain

Pain makes you stronger. Fear makes you braver.
Heartbreak makes you wiser.—Unknown

We can have both physical and mental pain. Most of us have pain and suffering in some form. We are either in the middle of a storm or waiting for one to happen.

Life can be unstable. Pain can also give us strength. We can learn from it and then move on. It's part of life.

Well everybody hurts, sometimes
Everybody cries,
Everybody hurts sometimes.

—REM

Feelings

Emotions are temporary states of mind.
Don't let them permanently destroy you.

—Unknown

Feelings come and go. They are not permanent. Just look and see how much they change during your day. The problem is, we keep feeding them, good or bad.

Sometimes we don't have any one particular emotion. Our minds are all over the place—not happy, not sad, not anything. Life can feel like one big blur. Just remember: no one can get inside your thoughts. Try not to let people control your feelings. Acknowledge your feelings and see why they are with you, and then act upon them.

These feelings won't go away, they've
been knocking me sideways.
I keep thinking in a moment that
time will take them away.

—*Citizen Cope*

Friendship

Friendship isn't about who you've known the longest.
It's about who walked into your life, said
"I'm here for you," and proved it.

—*Unknown*

Friendship is not about how many friends you have, it's about the ones who stick by you—the loyal ones and the ones you trust in good times and bad. Good hearts are hard to find, but they are out there. Good friends make you feel at ease. They respect you as you are. They are reliable in times of need and love. Choose wisely.

Winter, spring, summer, or fall
All you have to do is call
And I'll be there.

—James Taylor

Walk Away

Walk away from anything or anyone who takes away your joy. Life is too short to put up with fools.—Unknown

It's difficult to walk away sometimes. We like to cling even if it hurts. Being a good person does not mean people will always be good to you. You only have control over yourself. If you are not happy or are trying to hold on to someone who does not care or uses you, show courage and act upon it. It's your choice to accept people's behaviour or walk away.

It's so hard to do, and so easy to say,
But sometimes, sometimes you just have to walk away.

—Ben Harper

This Too Shall Pass

Remind yourself that this moment is temporary.
You are resilient and strong.
Everything changes.
This too shall pass.

—Unknown

Not everything we encounter in life will stay the same. Everything passes. Remember back when you were anxious or scared or uneasy about a particular situation? As time fades, the worries pass. Stop dwelling on what could have been or what could happen. This will pass.

Calm yourself and reassure yourself that the good and bad times will pass. Everything is temporary. Just say it over and over again when needed. It's the truth. This too shall pass, this too shall pass.

I've got to break free,
I want to break free,
I want, I want, I want,
I want to break free.

—Queen

Peace

Peace does not mean to be where there is no noise,
trouble, or hard work. It means to be in the midst of
those things and still be calm in your heart.—Unknown

Most of us wish for world peace—peace amongst all peoples. To accept our differences and live in harmony, we must find peace in ourselves and in our hearts first. The world can be in chaos and our minds as well. Practice peaceful thoughts. Be kind to others. We can all play our part. Love, peace, and happiness can win in the end. Let's try.

Oh peace train, sounding louder,
Glide on the peace train.
Come on now peace train.

—Cat Stevens

MUSIC ARTISTS QUOTED

Bryan Adams
Ryan Adams
The BoDeans
James Brown
Nenah Cherry
Citizen Cope
Coldplay
The Cranberries
Creedence
    Clearwater
    Revival
Sheryl Crow
Stephen Cummings
The Eagles
Steve Earle
Faith No More
Fleetwood Mac
Michael Franti
Ben Harper

The Hollies
Janet Jackson
Jason and the
    Scorchers
Jimmy Eat World
Jack Johnson
Howard Jones
Lenny Kravitz
John Lennon
Bob Marley
Alanis Morisette
Nine Inch Nails
No Doubt
Oasis
Roy Orbison
Plain White T's
Powderfinger
Queen
Red Hot Chili Peppers

Relient K
REM
Xavier Rudd
Joe Satriani
Seals and Croft
Paul Simon
The Smithereens
Bruce
    Springsteen
Cat Stevens
James Taylor
Rob Thomas
U2
Van Halen
Weird Al
    Yankovic
Kanye West
Lucinda Williams
Neil Young
The Youngbloods

Printed in the United States
By Bookmasters